Solveig Larsson's
Knitted Mittens

Solveig Larsson's Knitted Mittens

Over 40 Wearable Patterns
Inspired by the Landscape, Legends, and
Lasting Traditions of Northern Sweden

by Solveig Larsson

T

TRAFALGAR SQUARE
North Pomfret, Vermont

First published in the United States of America
in 2015 by
Trafalgar Square Books
North Pomfret, Vermont 05053

Originally published in Swedish as *Solveigs vantar – Inspiration från norr*.

The instructions and material lists in this book were carefully reviewed by the author and editor; however, accuracy cannot be guaranteed. The author and publisher cannot be held liable for errors.

ISBN: 978-1-57076-702-9

Library of Congress Control Number: 2014952915

Translation by Carol Huebscher Rhoades

Text: Solveig Larsson and Leif Larsson
Layout: Christina Snell-Lumio
Drawings: Leif Larsson
Photography: All photos by Leif Larsson, Solveig Larsson, and Lena Abrahamsson, except p. 21 (Kajsa Bremberg); p. 22 bottom (Margona Berggren); p. 46 (Viktor Åberg); p. 61 (Göran Wallin); p. 86 (Porjus Archive Committee); p. 106 left (Bengt-Göran Nilsson).

Printed in China

10 9 8 7 6 5 4 3 2 1

Table of Contents

Preface

The years of mitten knitting have been fun, and, most fun of all, the pattern drawing behind the 43 new designs presented here—so it is now time for a book, *Solveig Larsson's Knitted Mittens: Over 40 Wearable Patterns Inspired by the Landscape, Legends, and Lasting Traditions of Northern Sweden.* This book contains only mittens inspired by various people and places in northern Sweden.

There are some women that I will talk about without whom this book would not have been possible. Many of them had a hard life but, at the same time, they had the capacity to both see and create beautiful things that were useful and made people happy. They actively passed down pattern traditions to a younger generation.

I will also discuss the workhouses in Norrbotten, which were, during the early twentieth century, boarding houses for poor children and children with a long way to school. They were a form of relief during Sweden's years of famine at the beginning of the twentieth century. Coincidentally, they promoted cultural and historical work: Mittens and mitten patterns from homes and villages near the work-houses were collected by the children living there. Girls knitted and sold mittens to support the workhouses financially. That contributed both to the preservation of traditional patterns and to new creations.

Many of the mittens from the north are so-called band mittens. The pattern is worked in panels around the mittens, usually in strong colors. Sami shoe bands have obviously inspired these mittens, and they remain a great source of inspiration today.

For me, even nature is inspiring. I just have to think about being in the mountains in Björkliden holding a very small frog in my hand. What an experience! Of course, I've seen frogs before but never such a tiny one. That's how the design and mitten "The Frog" came about.

The basic instructions and patterns in this book assume that you have some knitting experience. The yarn I used for my mittens is 2-ply wool yarn purchased in skeins from various wool mills in Sweden. I've even used some handspun yarns.

My patterns are designed to work just as well with only black and white or with various colors. You can choose your own colors rather than those I used for knitting the mittens.

I hope that you, with the help of this book, will be inspired to knit and maybe even design your own patterns. Pattern charting is unbelievably fun and inspiring.

Choose a good quality yarn and the colors you like.

Good Luck!

Solveig Larsson

Abbreviations

CO	cast on	rem	remain(s) (ing)
dpn	double-pointed needles	rnd(s)	round(s)
k	knit	RS	right side
k2tog	knit 2 together	ssk	(slip 1 knitwise) 2 times, knit the 2
M1	make 1: lift strand between two		sts together through back loops.
	sts and knit into back loop	st(s)	stitch(es)
MC	main color	WS	wrong side
p	purl		

Basic Mitten Instructions

Mittens knit with 2-ply yarn

Yarn: 2-ply wool yarn
Needles: U.S. size 1-2 / 2.5 mm: set of 5 dpn

Pattern: Follow the chart.

Make sure that the floats on the wrong side are not too long. To prevent the mitten from puckering and avoid long strands that you might catch your fingers in, twist strands around each other every 2-3 stitches.

Mittens
CO 60 sts. Divide sts as evenly as possible onto 4 dpn. Join, being careful not to twist the cast-on row.
Work 6 rnds of garter stitch for bottom of cuff: (knit 1 rnd, purl 1 rnd) 3 times.
Now work following the pattern chart up to the thumbhole. The red lines on each chart show the placement of the right and left thumbholes.

Thumbhole: Use a smooth contrast color waste yarn to knit 13 or 12 sts. Slide the sts back to the left needle and knit again in pattern. Work approx. 32 rnds above thumbhole.

Top shaping:
Ndls 1 and 3: Ssk and then work to end of needle.
Ndls 2 and 4: Work across until 4 sts rem. K1, k2tog, k1 (edge st at end of needle).

Thumb: Carefully remove waste yarn from thumbhole. Pick up sts on the top and bottom of the thumbhole, with each set on a separate dpn: 13 - 13 or 12 - 12 sts. Now knit across first dpn, pick up and knit 2 sts at corner, work across next dpn and then pick up and knit 2 sts at corner = 13+2+13+2 for a total of 30 sts or 12+2+12+2 for a total of 28 sts.
Work in pattern for 19 rnds. Finish thumb tip as for top of mitten.

Second Mitten: Work as for first mitten, placing thumbhole on the opposite side of palm.

Finishing
Weave in all ends neatly on WS, making sure that ends at base of thumb and tip of mitten are well secured. If you would like to add a tassel to each mitten, sew it on securely now.

Wash the mittens in very warm water with wool-safe soap. Rinse in ice cold water, then in hot water; repeat once more.

Dry the mittens lying flat on a hand towel. When the mittens are completely dry, brush up the surface with a very stiff bristle brush. Brush the inside and the outside of each mitten.

Tassels
Wind some yarn over a few fingers held together—or your whole hand, depending on how long you want the tassel. Remove the yarn and secure the tassel with a strand tied at the top. Let this short strand hang loose. Wrap the tassel with the desired yarn color, as wide as you like, and then cut at the bottom.

Ylva wearing the Kalix mittens.

Techniques

Flat Decrease Shaping
Ndl 1: Knit the first 2 sts together as if knitting a regular knit stitch.
Ndl 2: Work across needle until 2 sts remain. Knit last 2 sts together through back loops (or ssk).
Ndl 3: Work as for Ndl 1.
Ndl 4: Work as for Ndl 2.

Two-Color Cast-On (see top left photo)
Make a slip knot loop with 2 colors of yarn. Cast on with long-tail cast on, holding one color over your thumb and the other over your index finger. The yarn over the thumb will form the lower edge. The color around the index finger will form the loops of the cast-on row.
Before you start knitting the first round, slide the slip knot off and leave it hanging. Later on, you can untie it and weave in ends on WS of mitten.

Estonian Kihnu Island Braid
(worked over 2 rnds) (see bottom left photo)
Round 1: Knit, alternating colors A and B around.
Round 1: Bring both strands to the front between the needles — both strands remain at the front throughout round. Purl around, alternating B and A (opposite colors of rnd below). Always bring the color to be used next *under* the previous color.

Two-End Purl Braid
Bring both strands to the front between the needles — both strands remain at the front throughout round. Bring the back yarn over the front one and purl the next st. Bring the next strand *over* the one just used and purl the next st. When returning to knit sts, move both strands to the back between the needles.

Double Start Cast-On

Begin as for a regular long-tail cast-on with a slip knot which will be Stitch #1.

To make Stitch #2, change the position of the yarn over your thumb, as shown in Drawing A below. Insert the needle below the strand on the inside of your thumb (the strand between the index finger and the thumb).

Catch the yarn around the index finger and then bring it back through the thumb loop—see Drawing B.

Drop thumb loop and tighten yarn for stitch. Return yarns to beginning position for long-tail cast-on.

There should now be 2 sts on the needle, Sts #1 and #2.

Continue the same way with St #3 as for regular long-tail cast-on.

St #4 is worked following Drawings A and B. Alternate sts cast on with long-tail method and method in Drawings A/B. Drawing C shows the pairs of stitches.

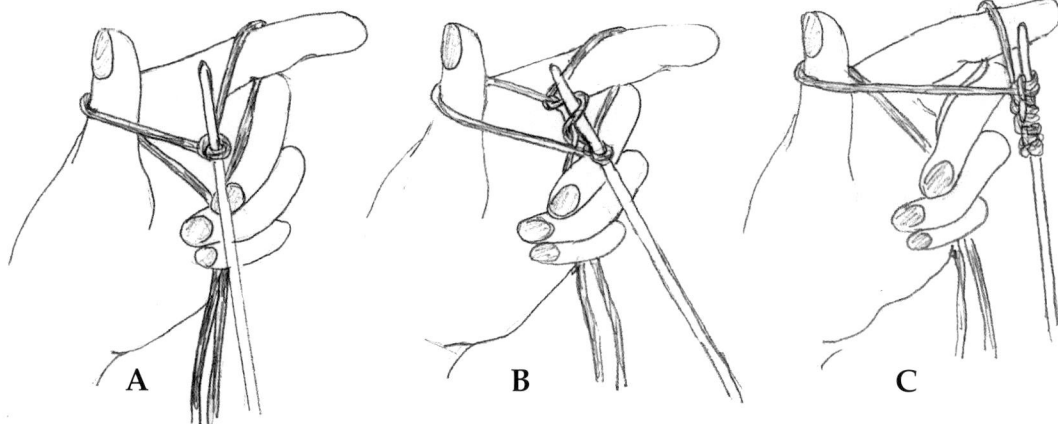

A   B   C

Töre Cuff (see photo to right)

CO 56 sts with the MC, as here, for example, black. Knit 1 rnd with black.

On the next rnd, begin working in k2, p2 ribbing. Add another color (we used purple).

Always work knit over knit and purl over purl while shifting the colors as follows:

Rnd 1: *K1 black, k1 purple, p2 black, k1 purple, k1 black, p2 purple*; repeat * to * around.

Rnd 2: *K1 purple, k1 black, p2 purple, k1 black, k1 purple, p2 black*; rep * to * around.

Repeat Rnds 1 and 2 for desired length. End with 1 knit round all in black.

Braid Cast-On (see photo to right)

Make a slip knot loop with Colors A and B and place on needle. Begin cast-on with A around your index finger and B around your thumb. Cast on 1 st as for regular long-tail cast-on. Now change position of yarns so A is around your thumb and B around the index finger. *Always* change colors to that the index finger yarn comes over the other strand.

Change colors after every stitch. This makes a decorative cast-on edge.

A handcraft class at Martingården in Överkalix, Sweden, 2012.

Adela

The subtle fall color scale at the lake inspired these mittens.

My mother-in-law was a productive knitter all year round. She mostly knit socks for
her children and grandchildren. Even after
she became blind when she was old, she
knitted. Every time we came on a visit, she
wanted me to pick up the stitches she had
dropped. Every summer, she spent most of
the time on the island on the other side of
the sound.

These mittens, Adela, are named for her.

Knitting Instructions: CO 60 sts with the two-color method (see Techniques, page 10).

Anna Teresia

Early in life, Anna Teresia had to take on great responsibilities. Her husband died when the oldest of their three children was only 4 years old. Thanks to knitting on a knitting machine, she was able to support herself, the children, and her sickly parents-in-law. At the home of her son Dan and his wife Inger in Tärendö, I saw many beautiful shoe ties, which inspired the Anna Teresia mittens.

ANNA TERESIA

Anna Karlsson she was called,
Anna Teresia,
the girl from Merasjärvi,
the youngest of eleven children.

In Sangis she became a housewife on a small farm
with three little children in close succession.
Her husband died when the oldest child was four.

Anna bought a knitting machine
and supported herself and her children.
She took care of her sick parents-in-law
and the farm with four cows.

After eleven years, she found fame
through a newspaper.
"The Women We Want to Commemorate"
    was the title of the article.
Anna smiled and went out to the cows in the barn.

From the poetry book The Crows Go in with Their Feet
by Leif Larsson.

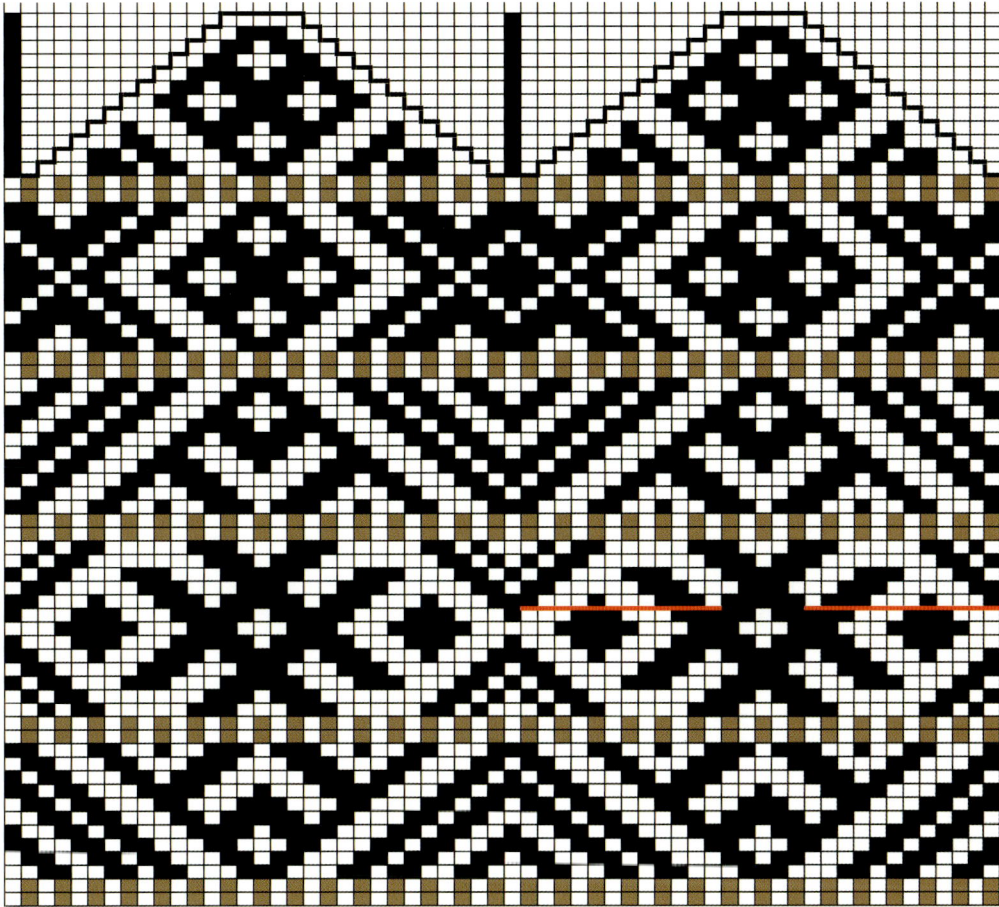

Knitting Instructions: CO 56 sts and work
cuff in k2, p2 ribbing.
On the first pattern round, increase to 60 sts
= (K14, M1) 4 times.
Continue, following the chart.

Arjeplog's workhouse

The Workhouses

For more than fifty years (up to the school year 1953/54), there were workhouses in Norrbotten and, in the beginning, in Västerbotten. Their intentions—to provide relief for poor children—were good, but many children did not consider their stay in the workhouses an easy time. Many have suppressed their experiences of those years, but some speak positively about their time in the workhouses.

In the summer of 1900, the crops didn't ripen; in 1901, the summer was dry and there was nothing to harvest. The winters of 1902 and 1903 were catastrophic for the people of Norrbotten. Hunger and deprivation were widespread. Many died, particularly children. There were many relief programs. Money was collected; food and other necessities were sent to Norrbotten and north Västerbotten. There wasn't any organized social assistance but funds were collected and dispersed to temporarily appointed persons.

The workhouses were a consequence of those difficult years. They were established by private initiative and had idealistic goals. Funds and contributions were raised from various foundations to sustain the workhouses. After a few years, the workhouses were awarded government support based on the number of children in each.

By 1903, 8 workhouses had been established where needs were considered most pressing. Four of them were situated in Finnish-speaking villages (Korpilombolo, Pajala, Pello, and Tärendö), and four in the Sami area (Arjeplog, Arvidsjaur, Gällivare, and Jokkmokk). The workhouses offered board and lodging for poor children and for children whose homes were a long way from any available school. The houses were located in each area's central town, where schools were nearby.

The authorities saw the workhouses as an important opportunity: The residents could be taught the Swedish language, Swedish manners, and Swedish customs. All conversations in the workhouses had to be in Swedish.

The goal of the workhouses' curriculum was to prepare children for adult life by teaching them handicrafts of various sorts. For the boys, it was primarily woodwork and shoe making. The girls learned the duties associated with care of the house and production of textiles.

For those of us who enjoy knitting and who like to vary the patterns for knitted garments, the workhouses are significant, even if this fact isn't always recognized. In many workhouses, children were assigned to collect patterns from home and from neighboring villages. These patterns were then shared among the workhouses and, in turn, inspired new patterns. Sales of the girls' knitted work and the boys' wood crafts generated income for maintaining the workhouses. At the same time, they supported cultural and historical preservation.

Arjeplog Mittens

Rich colors and small roses

Arjeplog mittens belong to the category often referred to as Sami mittens because they are from the Sami region. They are easy to recognize with their small roses and they are always knitted in bright colors, usually green, red, blue, yellow, and white.

The original source of inspiration was said to be rosepath woven goods.

The history of the Arjeplog mittens begins in the workhouse in that village. In 1903, the workhouse was opened for poor children or children who lived a long way from a school. The house was originally designed as a home for the elderly but became, instead, a workhouse for relief in a time of necessity and hunger at the turn of the 19th to 20th century.

Carin Bremberg is the name of one of our contemporary accomplished knitters from

Arjeplog. She wrote about her mother-in-law, Jenny Bremberg, who was born in 1914 and spent many years in the workhouse:

"Jenny was a clever knitter and learned to knit mittens with patterns. The children in the workhouse had to contribute to the maintenance of the home by knitting mittens to be sold. Jenny sold her mittens at the market square in Arjeplog. Another girl took her mittens to the Sami house, a home for Sami pensioners, and sold them for 5 Swedish crowns a pair. The mittens were very popular."

Early on, Jenny Bremberg knitted mittens with small roses in the pattern. Mittens with green backgrounds were for women and those with blue for men.

The Arjeplog mittens that are knitted these days have more variation in the pattern. The defining element remaining on all of them is the motif of little roses which should be knitted with three colors. The background color is also used for a dot at the center of each rose. These would be considered authentic Arjeplog mittens.

You can find examples of Arjeplog mittens at the Nordic Museum in Stockholm and in the Textile Collection in Sollefteå. At the Silver Museum in Arjeplog, there is an example of this in their large mitten collection, which has around 300 mittens.

Source: Carin Bremberg

Margona

The Margona mitten is a type of Arjeplog mitten. My aunt Sonja from Örnsköldsvik called them Lapp mittens.

Grandmother Ruth knitted a pair of these mittens in the 1950s when she was in her fifties. She was born in Harads, which did not have a workhouse but the pattern had wandered there. The mittens are now owned by Margona, the daughter of my cousin in Örnsköldsvik.

I have knitted my own Margona mittens, following my grandmother's pattern but with other colors.

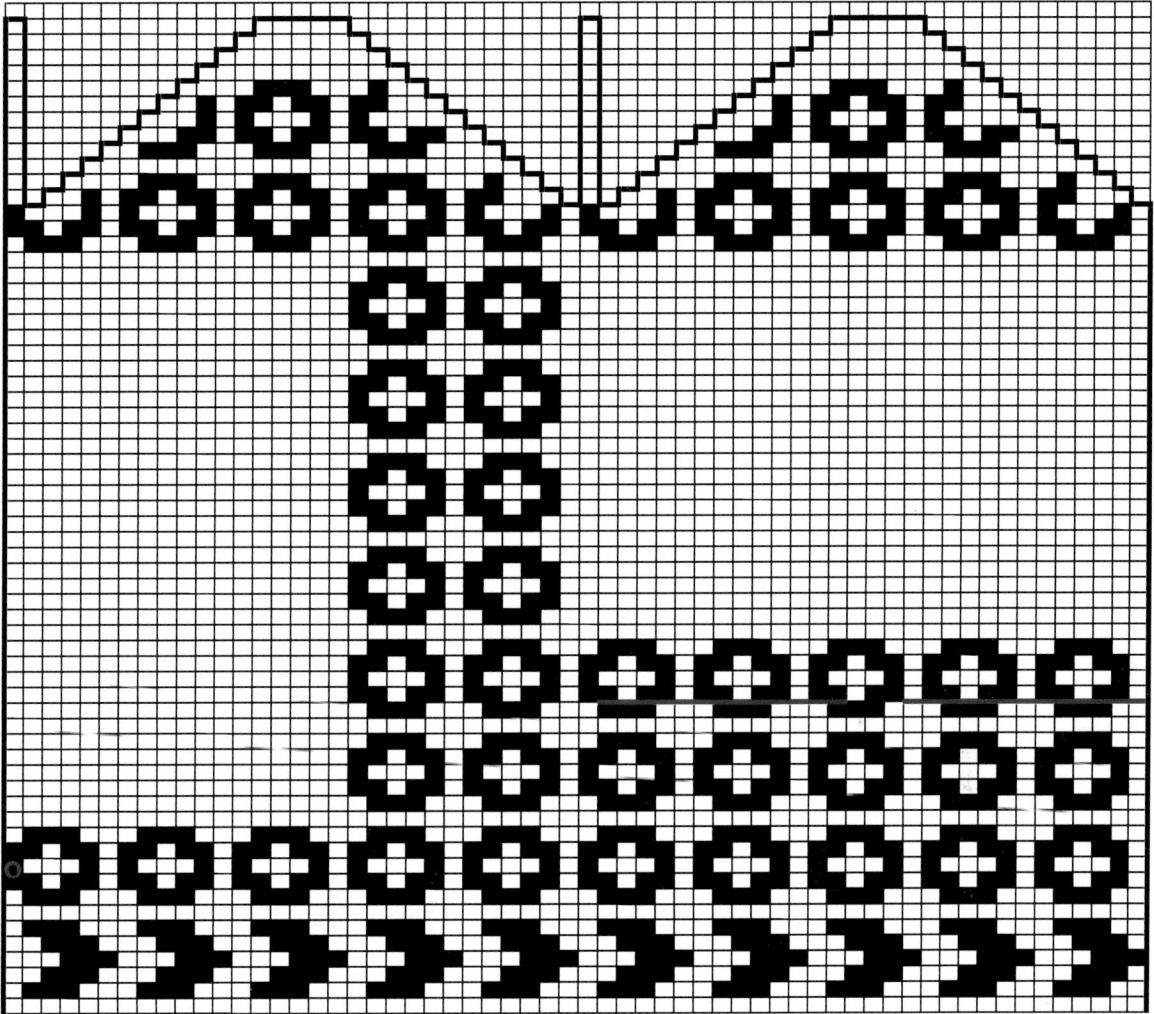

Knitting Instructions: CO 56 sts and work cuff in k2, p2 ribbing.
On the first pattern round, increase to 60 sts = (K14, M1) 4 times.
Continue, following the chart.

Margona

Aunes

The name Aunes is Sami and means Agnes. It was also used as a family name. In Övertorneå, there is, for example, a folk museum called Aunesgården.

Sami craft workers carve fine patterns on knife shafts and brooches. Their lovely carvings gave me the idea for the Aunes mitten pattern.

Knitting Instructions: See Basic Mitten Instructions, page 8.

Björkliden

The mountainous area of Sweden always provides recreation and inspiration. Every fall, we travel up to Björkliden, which is almost at the very northern tip of Sweden. The vistas looking out toward the Sami area give one a wonderful feeling.

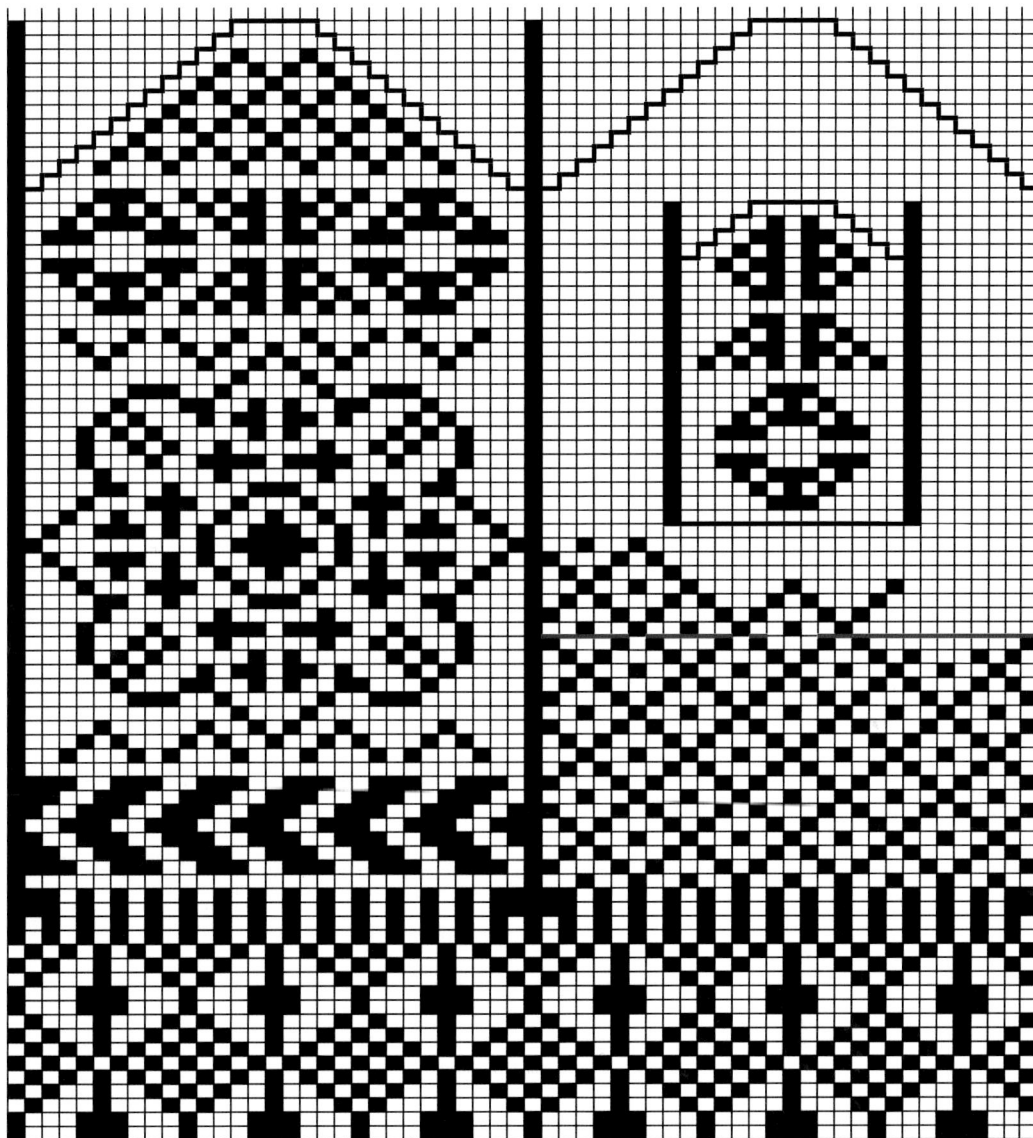

Knitting Instructions: Two-color cast-on (see Techniques, page 10).

Bluebells

Flowers and other plants are always a source of inspiration.

Knitting Instructions:
Begin with two-color cast-on (see Techniques, page 10). If you want green at the lower edge, hold the green strand around your thumb when casting on.

Next, *knit 1 rnd black, purl 1 rnd black; knit 1 rnd green, purl 1 rnd green. Rep from * once more.

Continue in pattern and form the top with flat shaping (see Techniques, page 10).

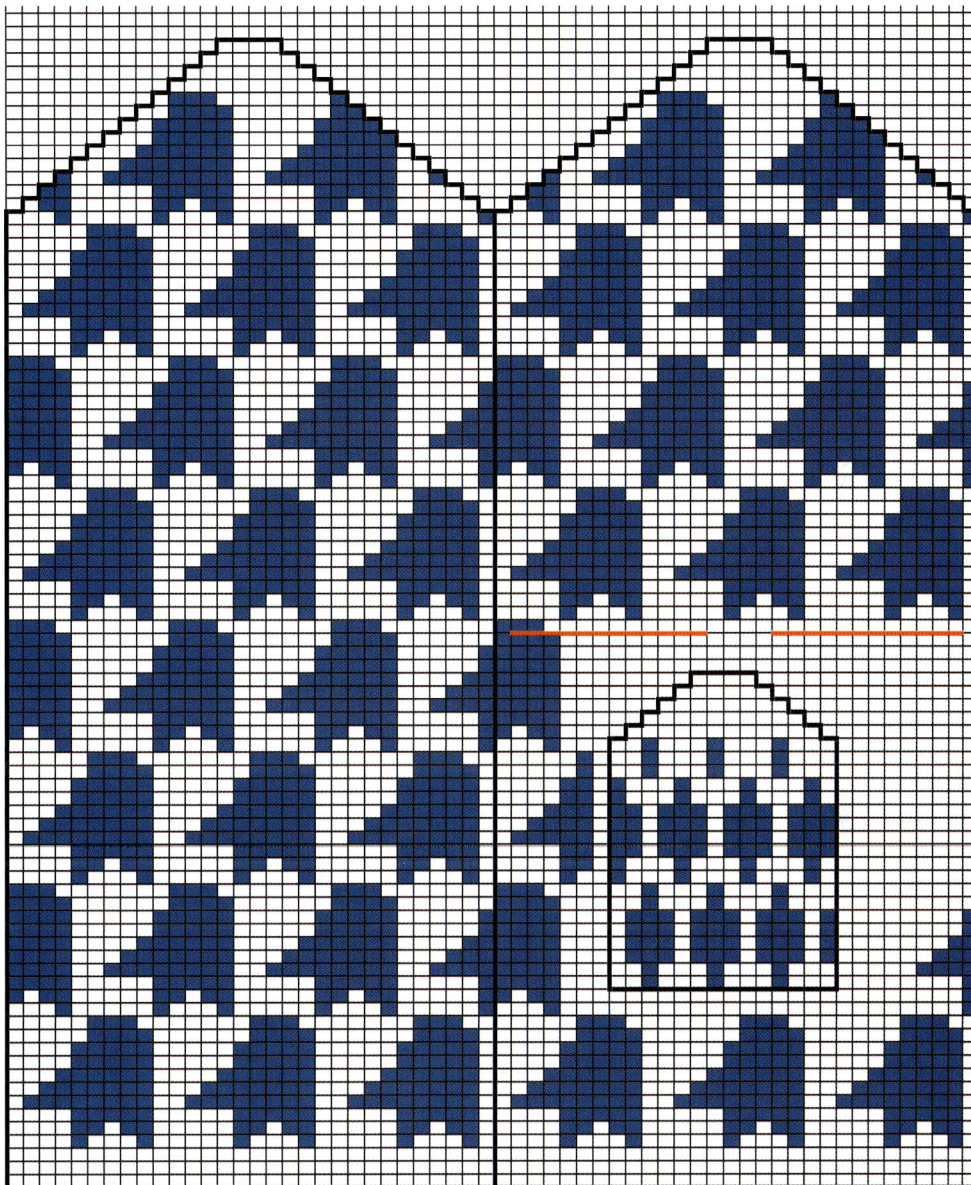

Knitting Instructions: See Basic Mitten Instructions, page 8.

Britta's Mittens

A curtain over the door at my friend Britta's house in Råneå led me to knitting the Britta mittens. Britta's mother had embroidered the pattern and Britta herself crocheted the lower section.

For the cast-on, I used my mother's gold yarn and white mohair.

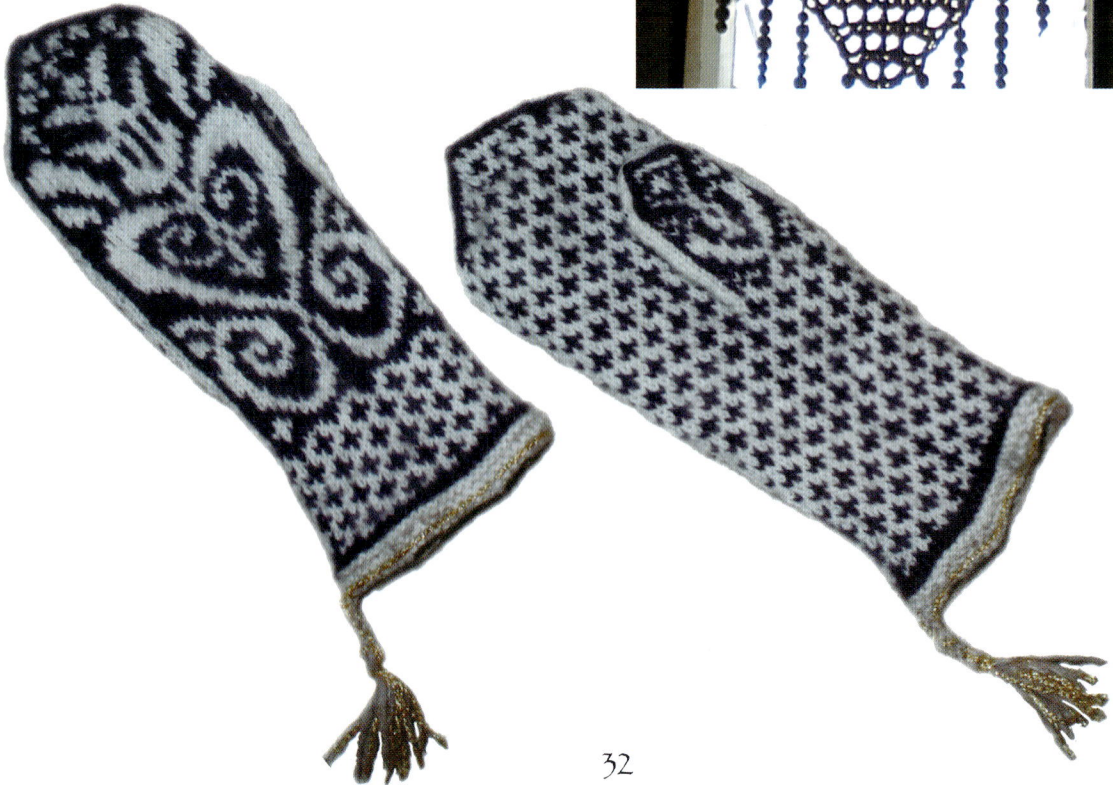

Knitting Instructions: See Basic Mitten Instructions, page 8.

Cyclamen

These mittens were inspired by a mini-cyclamen at home on the table in the living room. Johanna Brunsson's large pattern collection contains some similar patterns. These mittens are #9 in my Johanna Brunsson collection.

Knitting Instructions: See Basic Mitten Instructions, page 8.

Elli

Sami shoe bands always offer inspiration with endless possibilities for variations.

simple
Kihnu
braid

Knitting Instructions: CO 60 sts with the two-color method. Work following the charted pattern. Note the Estonian Kihnu braid at the wrist (see Techniques, page 10).

Eva's Mittens

Knitting Instructions: See Basic Mitten Instructions, page 8.

Mountain Avens

Unfortunately, the mountain avens had finished blooming by the time we visited Björkliden. Still, the plants were very pretty.

Knitting Instructions: See Basic Mitten Instructions, page 8.

Engagement Mittens

This flax or spinning wheel distaff, which I photographed at an exhibit in Norrbotten's museum, was produced in Norrbotten. Distaffs used to be given as an engagement gift. A typical flax distaff has notches to catch the fiber so it is at hand to be spun into yarn on the spinning wheel. The beautifully carved pattern was my inspiration for the Engagement Mittens.

Knitting Instructions: CO 60 sts with the double start cast-on (see Techniques). Work the garter stitch (alternate knit and purl rounds) lower edge and then follow the charted pattern.

The Frog

The little frog in my hand was also in my thoughts as I knitted these mittens with a frog motif.

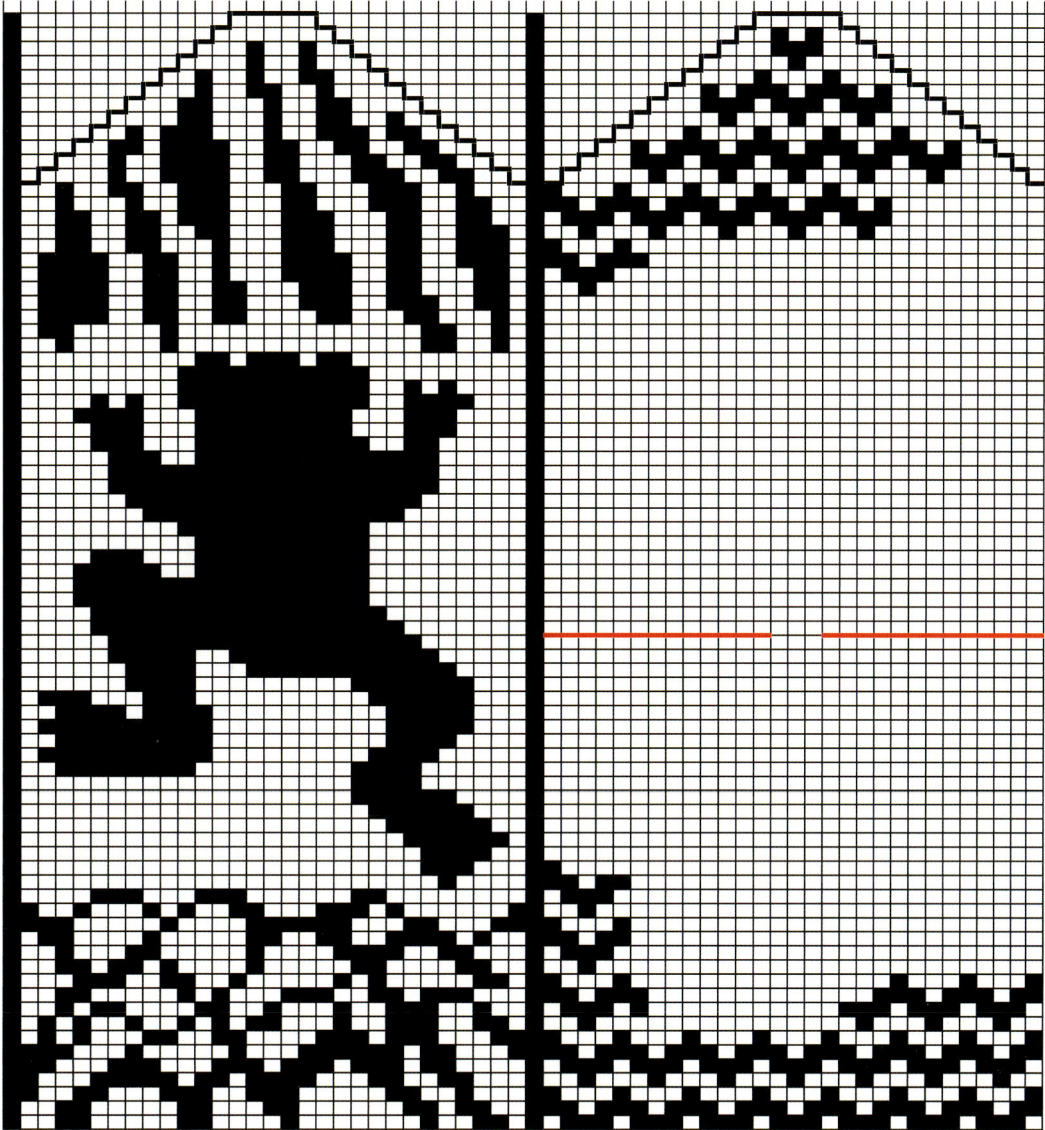

Knitting Instructions: Begin with two-color cast-on (see Techniques, page 10).

Gällivare

These mittens are knit in the bright colors typically used by the Sami. To the left of the mittens is my doll cradle, which I got when I lived for a short time in Gällivare. It was the first piece in my little Lapp lodge. A *komsio* is a Sami cradle that can be hung up.

Killinge Sami camp in the 195(

Dundret (a ski and conference resort in Gällivare), 1960. My brother Thomas and me.

Knitting Instructions: CO 56 sts and work in k2, p2 ribbing for the cuff. On the first pattern row after the ribbing, increase to 60 sts: (K14, M1) 4 times.

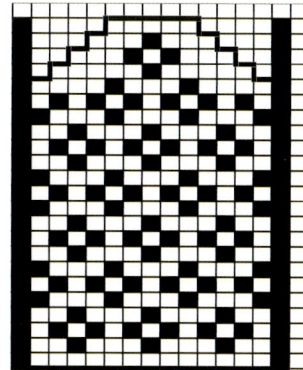

Hedgehog

The hedgehog in the picture was made by the ceramicist Tora Ceder.

For many years, we've noticed hedgehogs where we live. We've seen them play, wander around our yard, and take hazardous walks across the street. Hedgehogs are said to be one of the oldest still-living species of mammal.

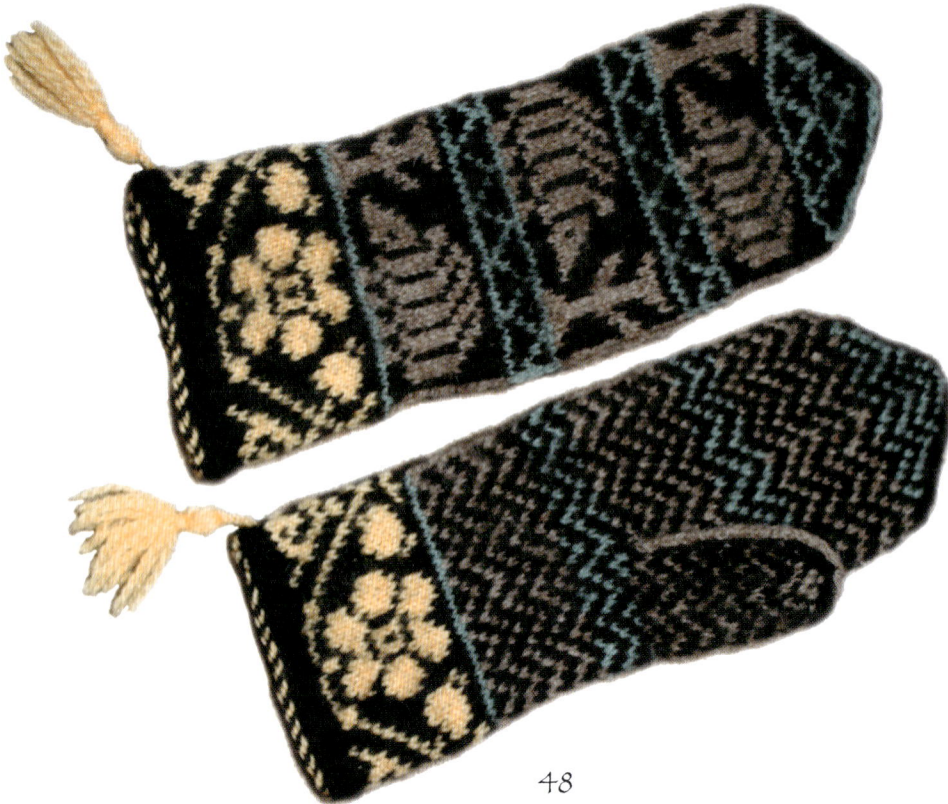

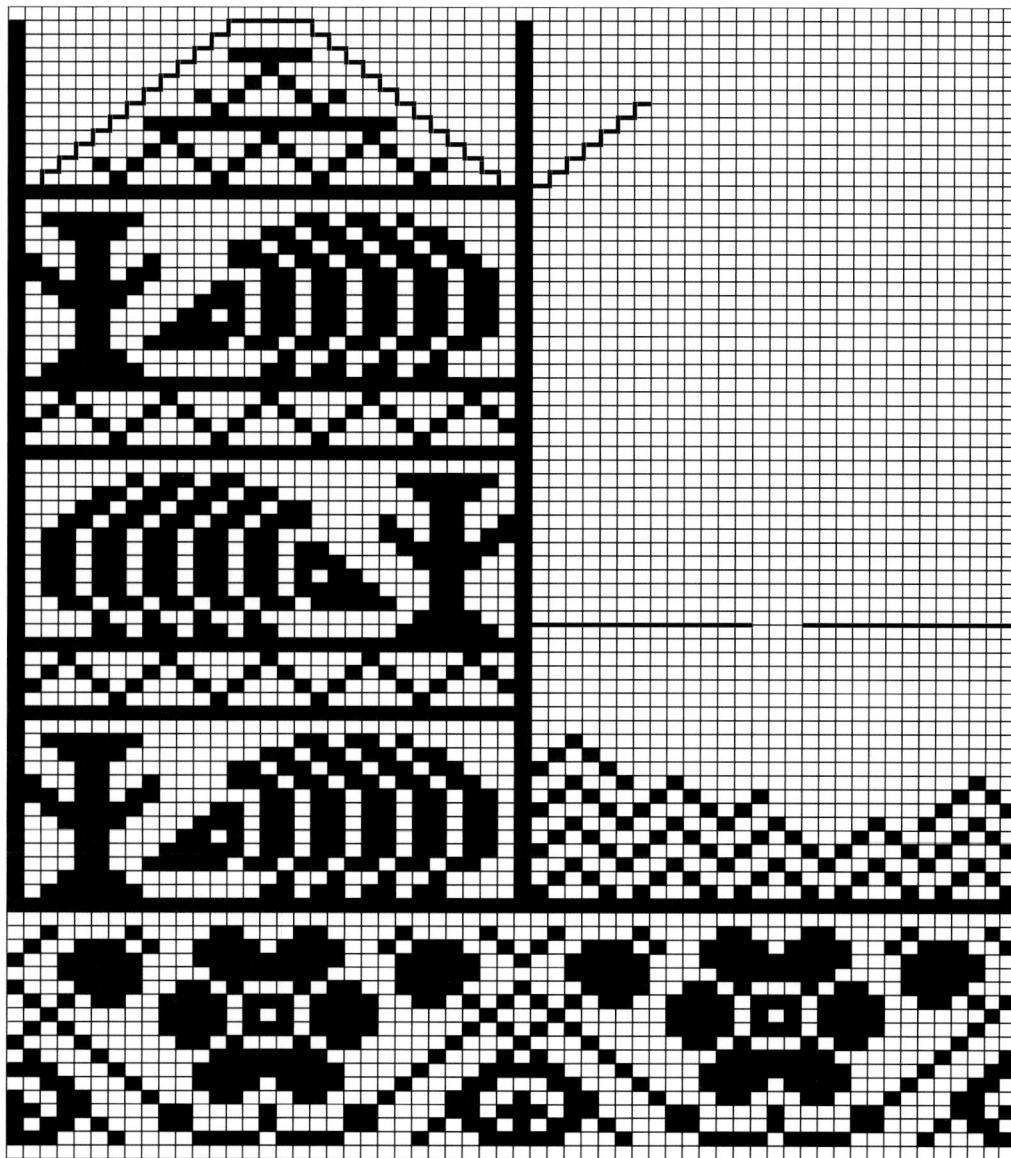

Knitting Instructions: Using braid cast-on method (see Techniques, page 12), CO 60 sts and then work following the chart (see Basic Instructions, page 8).

Jukkasjärvi Mittens

The itinerant school teacher Terese Torgrim collected pattern-knitted mittens from all the places where she worked. She collected mittens so that the girls she taught would have patterns to knit with connections to the village. I have seen Terese's mitten collection — it is magnificent!

Some years ago, I got an old ditto sheet with a mitten pattern entitled Jukkasjärvi, and I used it as the basis for my Jukkasjärvi mittens. Terese knitted similar mittens that she often gave away as presents.

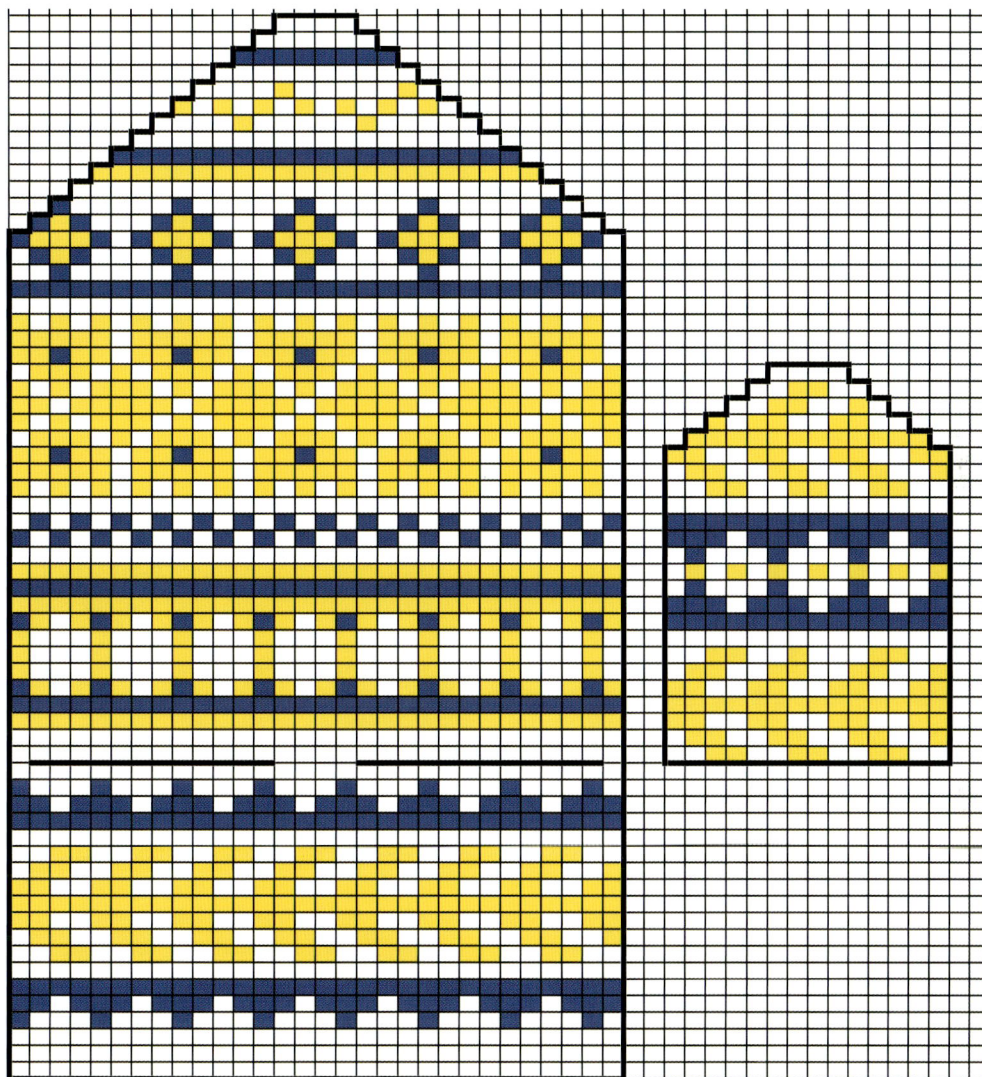

Knitting Instructions: CO 56 sts and work a k2, p2 ribbed cuff. On the first charted row, increase evenly spaced around to 60 sts (K14, M1) 4 times.

Katarína

Martingården in Överkalix is one of Sweden's best preserved folk life museums from the eighteenth century. It is a typical Norrbotten estate with buildings all around and interiors filled with many pieces of folk-art painted furniture.

Bottom photo at right: An old cheese form that inspired the pattern for these mittens.

Knitting Instructions: CO 54 sts with simple braid cast-on (see Techniques, page 12) and then work a Kihnu braid over two rounds (see Techniques, page 10). Next, work 16 rnds (k1 black, k1 white) around and then work following the chart.

The
Crown

Knitting Instructions: See Basic Mitten Instructions, page 8.

Lapland Heather

Lapland heather, as well as other types of heather, is very common in the fells of Björkli-den. The heather grows to about 4-8 in / 10-20 cm and blooms in July.

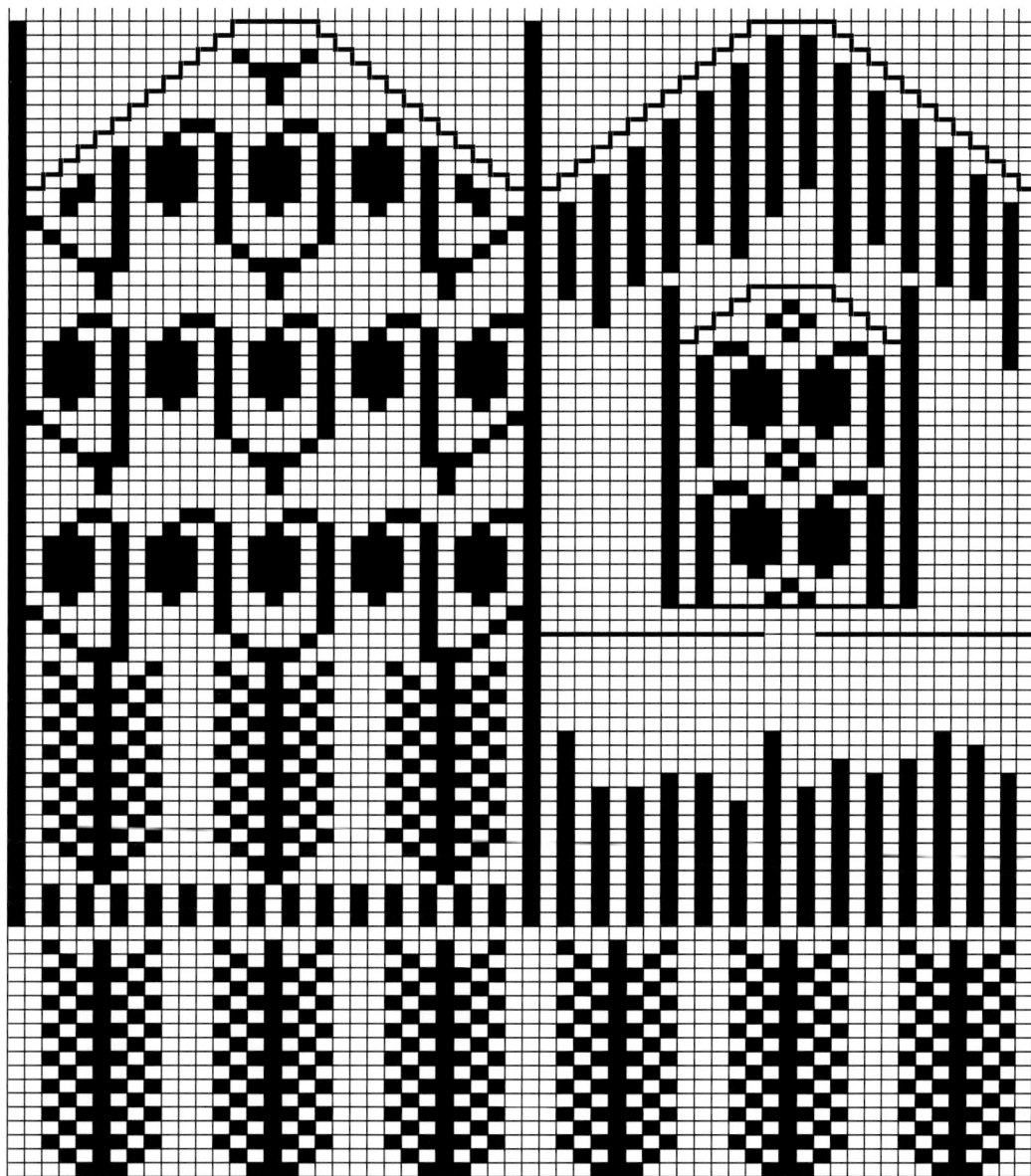

Knitting Instructions: CO 60 sts with the braid cast-on (see Techniques, page 12).

Linda

These mittens feature bands of patterns all around the hand.

Knitting Instructions: With the two-color method (see Techniques, page 10), CO 56 sts, holding the black yarn over your index finger. Knit 1 rnd and then work the Töre cuff (see Techniques, page 12). Finish cuff with 1 rnd in gray and then work mitten hand following charted pattern.

Lisa Zetterström

Skåne-Dalecarlian Woman in Vistasdalen

In a roadless landscape in Vistasdalen, about 9 miles / 15 km north of Nikkaluokta, there is a little cottage that is always open. It is "Lisa's Cottage," only 9 x 8 feet / 3 x 2.5 m. You can even find the name on the fell maps. The cottage is named for Anna Elisabeth Zetterström, who was one of the very few private people allowed to build in this mountain region.

Lisa Zetterström, who was born in Dalarna (central Sweden), worked as a nurse in Skåne (southwest tip of Sweden) but, during her wanderings in the mountains, fell in love with Vistasdalen. In 1932, she obtained permission to build her cottage. Per Sarri cut the wood for the building and drove the pieces to the site by horse and sled. Twice a year, she visited her cottage to enjoy the quiet and renewal that the mountain landscape gave her. She visited at Easter time and in the summer. The cottage was very small but well-equipped, and when she wasn't there others wandering in the mountains could stay there. At the end of the 1940s, Lisa Zetterström's visits to the cottage came to an end but she left all her personal belongings there for others to use. Lisa died on March 16, 1979, when she was almost 90 years old.

Norrbotten Province's Handcraft Consultant, Maud Ån, has visited Lisa's cottage several times since 1981. Unfortunately, she could prove that much of what had been in the cottage wasn't there any longer, and every year, more and more of Lisa's belongings disappeared. This included textiles and other handmade items. Finally, only one of Lisa's weavings was left—a dirty, rat-eaten wall hanging stuffed into the wood pile. Maud took it with her to show the county authorities; she lodged a request that they restore the cottage and ensure that it had frequent supervision.

I was able to see the wall hanging. Judging by the color combinations and motifs, it was likely woven with a pattern originally from Skåne. The wall hanging inspired me to design two pairs of mittens: Lisa and Lisa Z.

The pencil drawing above was done freely after a little picture in the Kiruna newspaper and is not necessarily an accurate portrait.

Sources: Handcraft Consultant Maud Ån; the Kiruna newspaper (a monthly magazine).

Maud Ån standing in the doorway of Lisa's cottage, holding Lisa's wall hanging.

Photo: Göran Wallin

Lisa Z

I made a fine braid and used a tapestry needle to thread it around the mitten. I then attached the tassels to the braid ends.

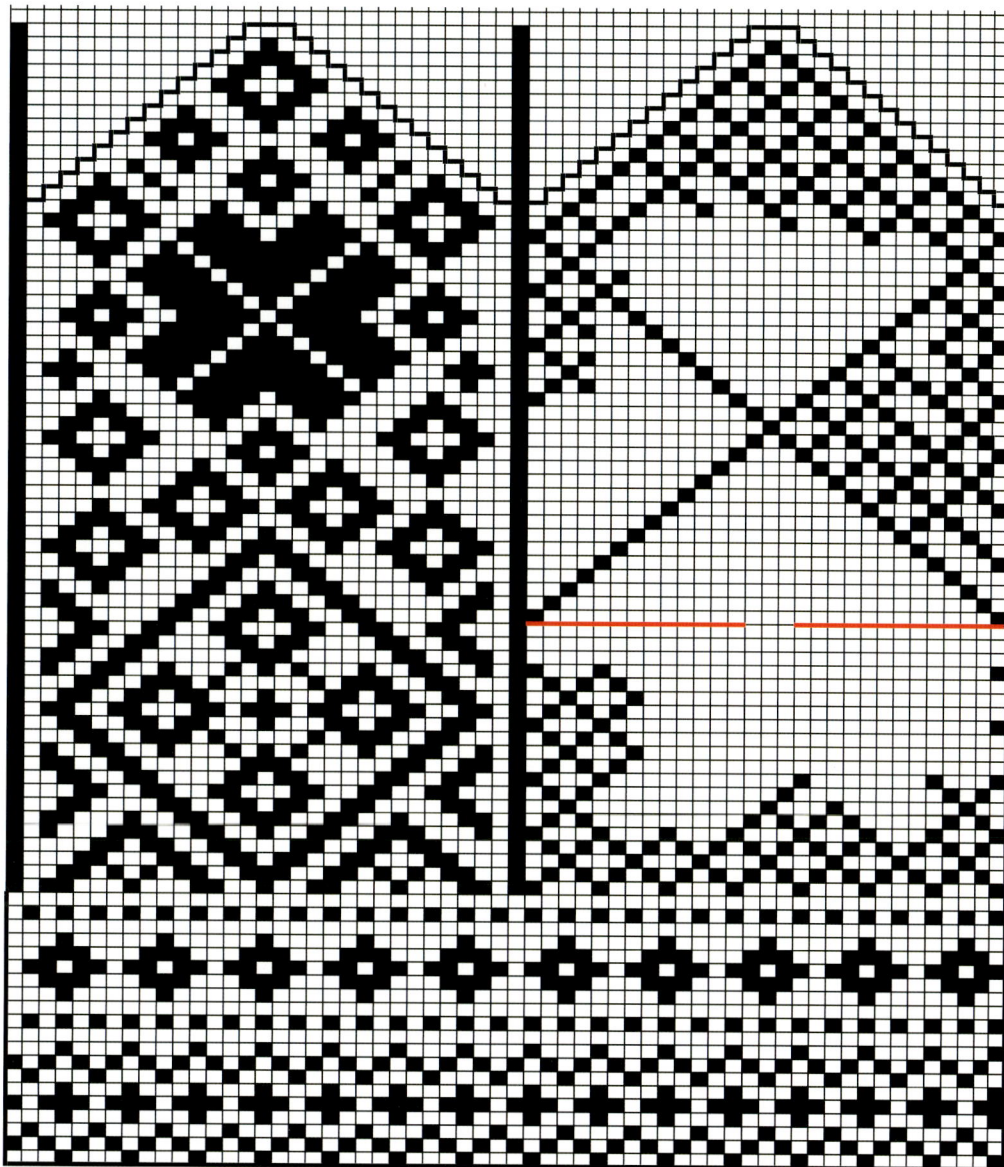

Knitting Instructions: See Basic Mitten Instructions, page 8.

Lisa

Knitting Instructions: See Basic Mitten Instructions, page 8.

Heather

Heather is a very common plant in the
north. It grows on both dry and damp
landscapes. The flowers bloom in Au-
gust and September. The leaves look
like needles and are green year-round.

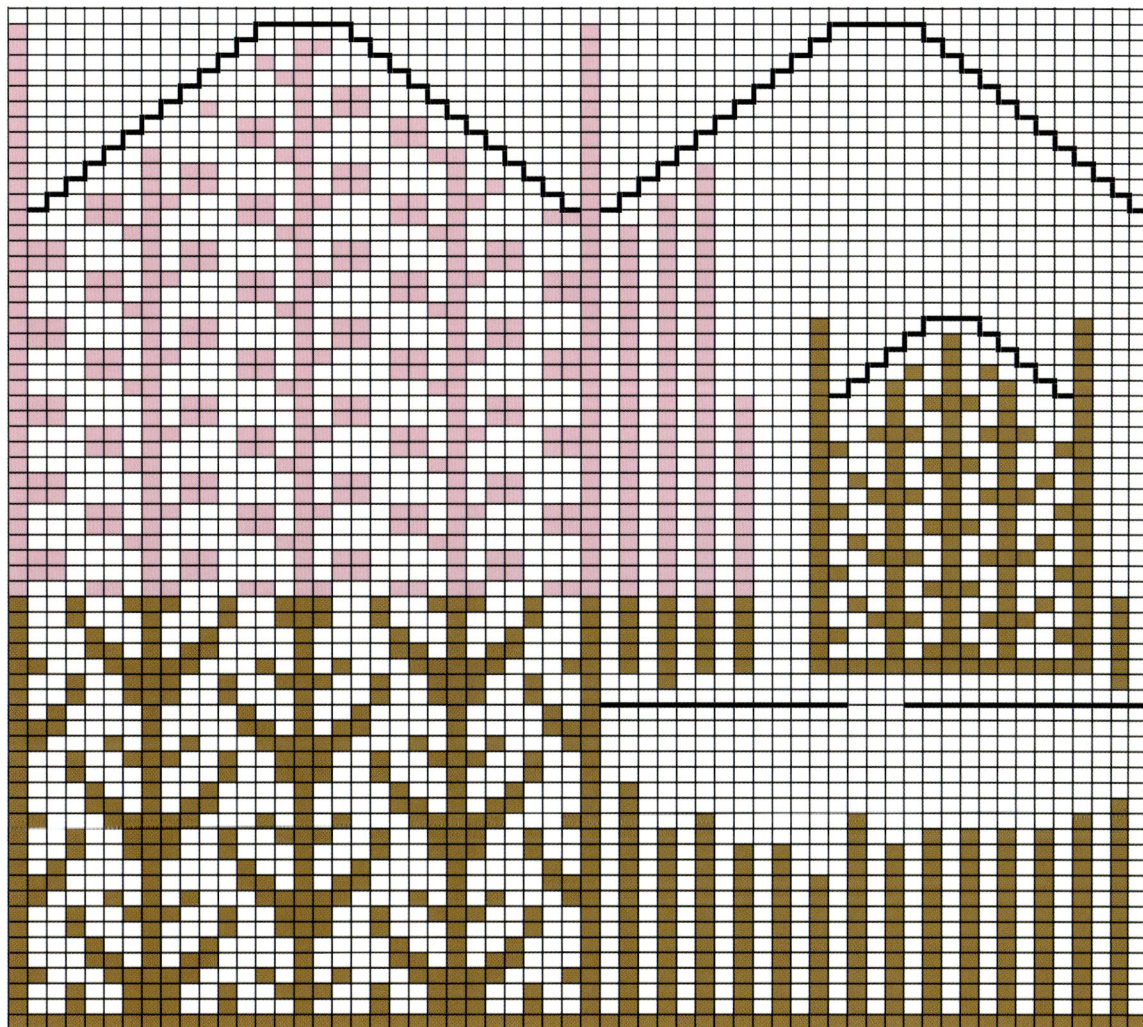

Knitting Instructions: Using the two-color method, CO 56 sts (see Techniques, page 10). Knit 1 rnd black and then purl 1 rnd in two-end purl braid, alternating black and pink yarn (see Techniques, page 10). Knit 1 rnd black and then work in k2, p2 ribbing for cuff. On the first row of the charted pattern, increase evenly spaced around to 60 sts: (K14, M1) 4 times.

Maple

Fall is a beautiful time of year that is very conducive to knitting. The air is chilly, clear, and clean, and the colors are lovely. You can't miss the large maple leaves, on the trees or on the sidewalk.

I once received a birthday present of a napkin holder with napkins patterned with maple leaves, and it wasn't long before I designed these maple mittens.

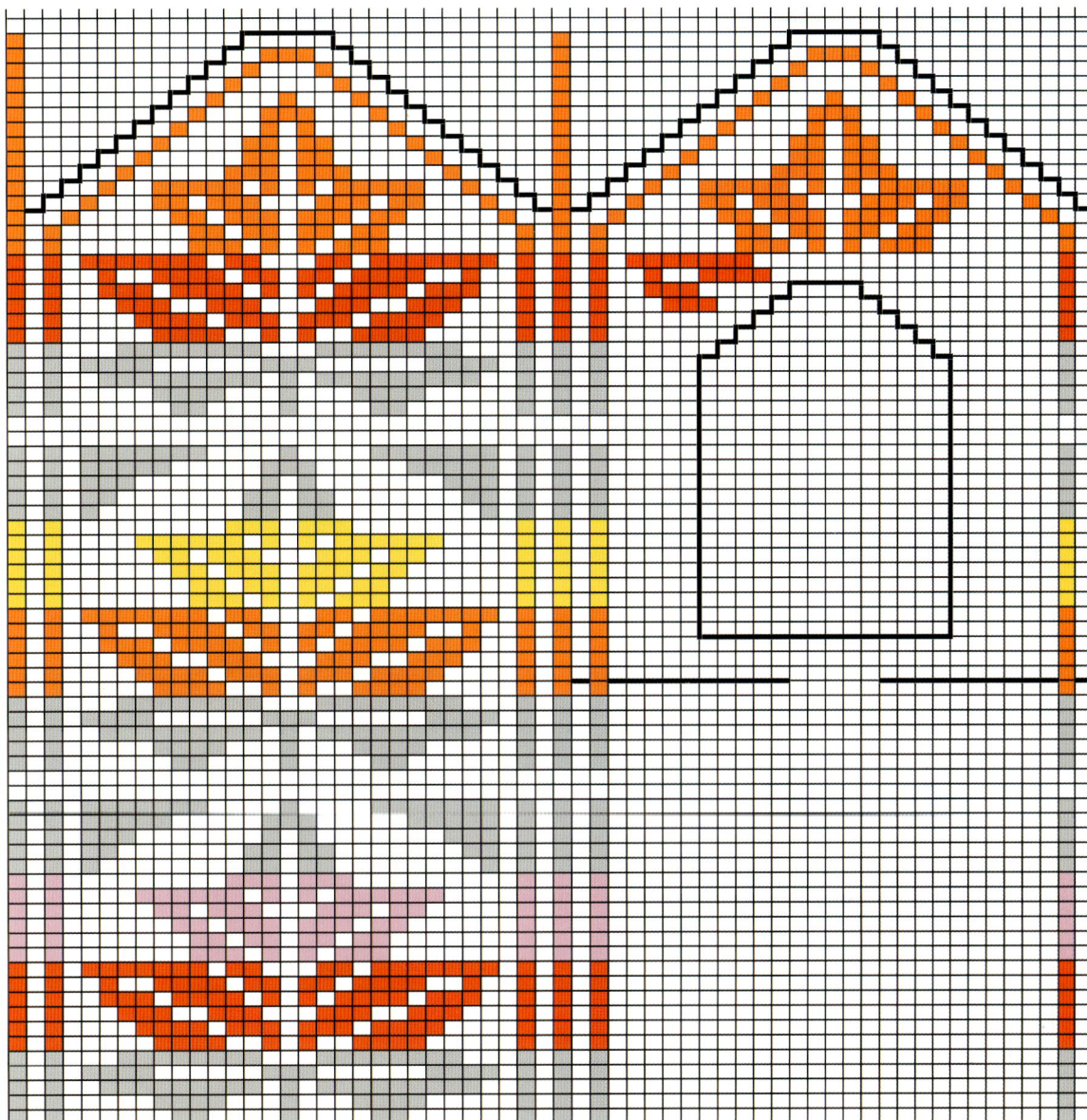

Knitting Instructions: See Basic Mitten Instructions, page 8.

Maja

A banded mitten with the pattern all the way around.

Old-fashioned raking at the Hägnan Open Air Museum.

Knitting Instructions: Knit a design you like for the thumb.

*My little brother, fishing on
the ice outside Norra Harbor
in Luleå in 1960.*

Majorov

It was actually a cap worn by an ice fisherman that inspired the pattern drawing for
these mittens. I named the mitten after the
very accomplished Luleå figure skater, Majorov, who was one of Sweden's elite. I later
found out that the ice fisherman in the lovely cap out on the ice was Majorov's father.

Knitting Instructions: See Basic Mitten Instructions, page 8.

Nestor

*The uppermost villag[e]
the Råneå river valley*

It's not just the so-called Lapland mittens that are colorful. You can find similar mittens in other parts of northern Sweden. These mittens have pattern bands covering the hands.

Ylva, our photo model, at 2½ years old.

74

Knitting Instructions: Using 3 colors (red; yellow; and blue, indicated by black on the chart), CO 56 sts. Hold the blue yarn over your index finger and the other two colors on your thumb. This will make blue loops on the needle. Knit 1 rnd with blue and then work in k2, p2 ribbing. Finish cuff with 1 knit rnd with blue, increasing at the same time to 60 sts: (k14, M1) 4 times.

I have marked off the various pattern panels with dotted lines across the chart.

Norrbotten
Star Mittens

Banded mittens with pattern motifs all the way around.

Knitting Instructions: See Basic Mitten Instructions, page 8.

Gerhard Larsson on a coffee break from berry picking.

Ottilia

The idea for these mittens came from an embroidered coffee table cloth from the 1950s. It was placed under a large cake stand. The tablecloth was white with white motifs. I decided to make the mittens with white and blue to match the coffee cup.

Knitting Instructions: Using the two-color method, CO 52 sts (see Techniques, page 10). Work the cuff in k2, p2 ribbing and then follow the charted pattern. As you start the hand, decide where you want to place the thumb gusset.

Frost-nipped ox-berries.

Pía

Knitting Instructions: See Basic Mitten Instructions, page 8.

Pirjo

These large grass tussocks are located near the village of Lovikka. Some people refer to them as skulls and others call them Cossacks' heads. Maybe they are thinking of the big bearskin caps that the Cossacks used to wear.

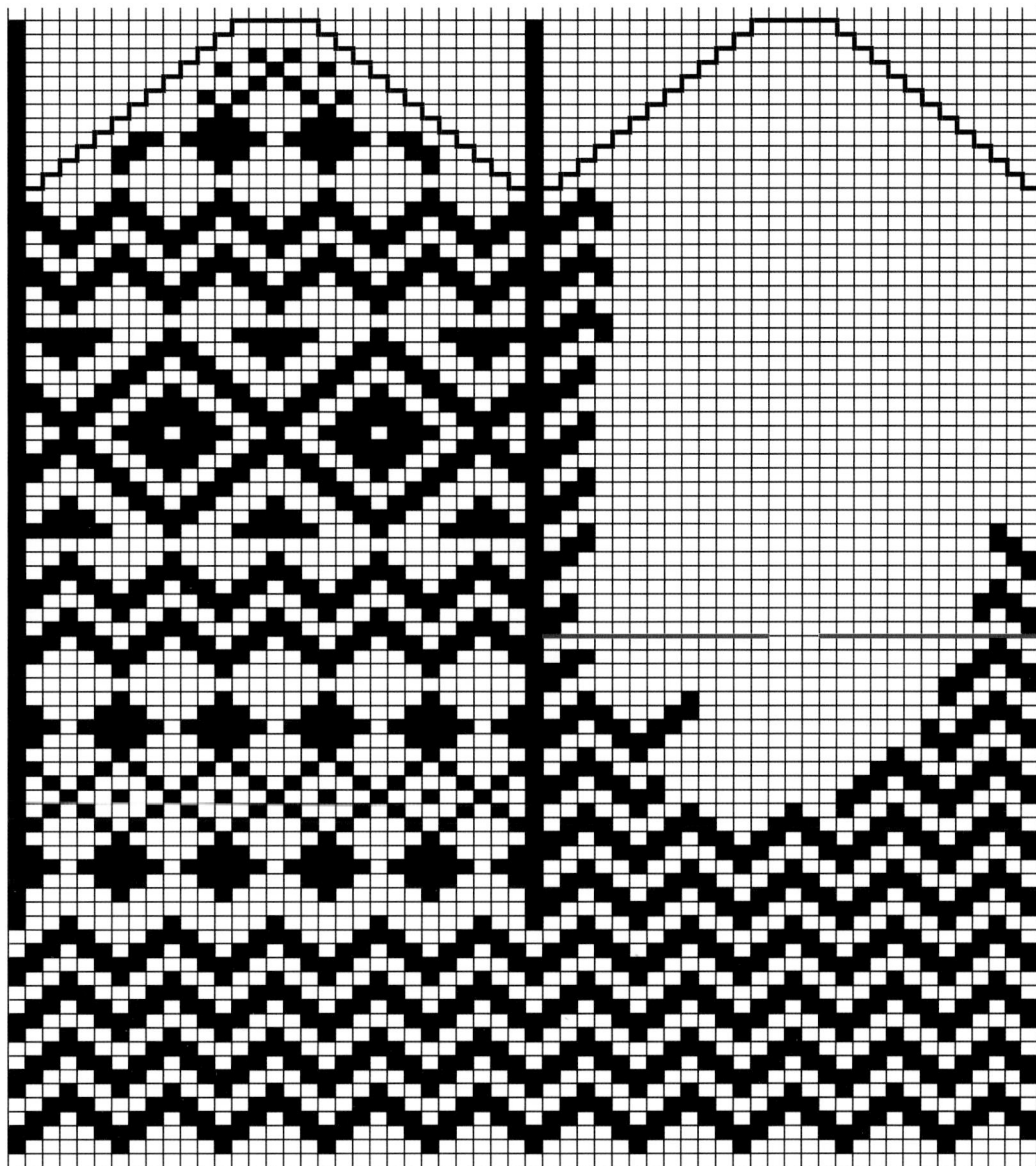

Knitting Instructions: See Basic Mitten Instructions, page 8.

Polar Nights

In the handcraft studio in Umeå, they used to weave damask tablecloths in the 1930s. The director of the program, Therese Årre, composed the cloth pattern "Reindeer Crown" from a Sami pattern. It was used both for tablecloths and furnishing fabric. I've reworked the design and called it "Polar Nights."

Knitting Instructions: CO 56 sts; join and work 5 rnds of k2, p2 ribbing. Next, knit 1 rnd, increasing to 60 sts: (k14, M1) 4 times. Continue, following the charted pattern.

Maria Juni's Porjus Mittens

Photo: Porjus Archive Committee

Hard life circumstances and events can also lead to preserving pattern traditions. Maria Juni from Porjus is a fine example of this.

The neighboring villages of Puoltikasvaara and Skaulo are located right between Gällivare and Kiruna. On November 9, 1888, Maria Olofsson was born in Puoltikasvaara. When she was old enough, she worked as a maid, first in Gällivare, then in Abborrträsk near Arvidsjaur, and later in Porjus. It was there that she met Oskar Henriksson Juni, who became her husband the day before Christmas Eve in 1910. Oskar worked as a power station builder and Maria was left alone for long periods, and had to be responsible for all the work at the house. Her life was simple and poor and the upbringing for the family's nine children rested on her shoulders for the most part. Three of the children died early from the scourge of that time: consumption.

1923 was a bleak year and there wasn't even enough money for milk. While gathering firewood from the forest, Maria sat down on a stone to rest and happened to see an old mitten on the ground near the stone. Although it was torn and dirty, she noted its red and yellow colors. Maria knitted a pair of mittens that looked like the one she had found. Her daughter, Berta, organized a lottery and went around to the neighboring houses selling tickets for the mittens. That was how the family earned enough money to buy milk.

These Porjus mittens, which often have the name Porjus and the year knitted in, were much sought after, and Maria Juni was able to contribute to the family income. She continued to knit tirelessly until she was very old, and more than ever after she became a pensioner, although she had decided to quit knitting at that point. On July 10, 1982, she died in Porjus when she was 94 years old. She wasn't able to complete her last pair of mittens, but others have continued her pattern tradition. It has been said that there is no longer anyone in Porjus who knits the Porjus mittens to sell.

Sources: Längs stigarna [Along the Path] *by Hans Andersson;* Maria Juni *by Lester Wikström*

New Porjus

Here's how I made my Porjus mittens.

Knitting Instructions: CO 56 sts and work cuff in k2, p2 ribbing.
On the first round after the ribbing, increase to 60 sts: (K14, M1) 4 times. Now follow the charted pattern. Form the top of the hand with flat decrease shaping (see Techniques, page 10). Finish the thumb tip the same way.

Reindeer
Mittens

Many tourists stop by
the road and take pic-
tures of the reindeer.
I also do that sometimes.

Knitting Instructions: See Basic Mitten Instructions, page 8.

Rowan

Knitting Instructions: With the double start method, CO 60 sts (see Techniques). Knit 1 rnd, purl 1 rnd, knit 2 rnds and then purl 1 rnd. Continue, following the charted pattern.

Selet

Sometimes we visit the Selet factory outside
Luleå and admire the lovely natural scenery
around the factory. We like to have coffee
and sandwiches there.

One time we were at a Kalix family gathering and heard a very interesting lecture
on the history behind the Selet factory. The
factory was established by Gustaf Hermelin,
and in 1799, the blast furnace was ready. Af-
terwards the business had many owners. In
1979, it became a nature reserve. In the room
where we sat and listened to the lecture,
there was some lovely wallpaper that gave
me the idea for the Selet mittens.

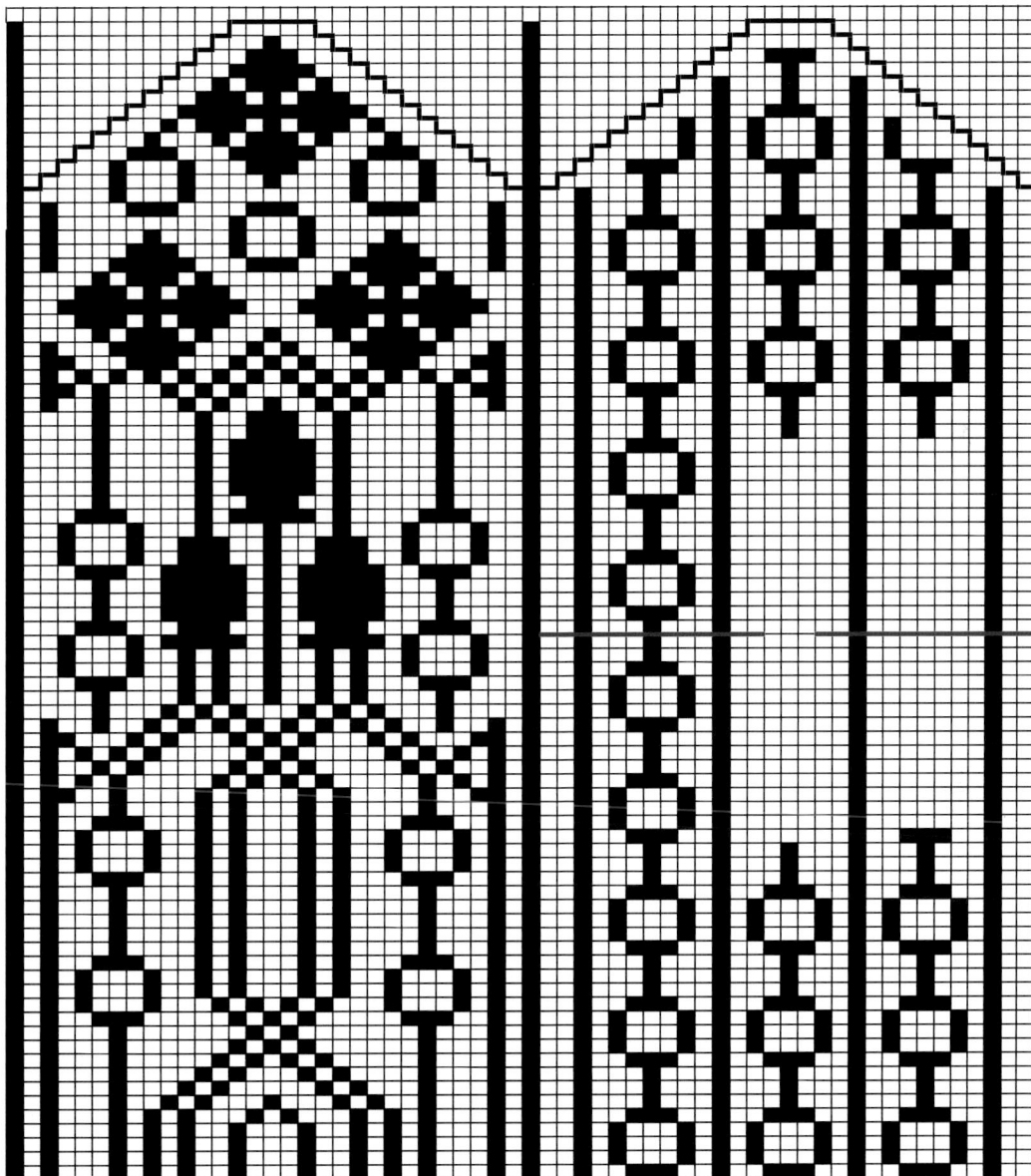

Knitting Instructions: See Basic Mitten Instructions, page 8.

Summer

Up here in the north of Sweden, summer is short but light-filled. Most people try to spend as much time as possible outdoors. I usually sit in the hammock and knit or read. This photo shows the view I usually have.

Kihnu braid

Knitting Instructions: Using the two-color method, CO 60 sts (see Techniques, page 10). Work a narrow garter st band (alternating knit and purl rnds) and then work following the chart. Note the Kihnu braid at the wrist (see Techniques, page 10).

Lousewort

Knitting Instructions: With white and black, using the double start method, CO 60 sts (see Techniques, page 11). With white only, knit 1 rnd, purl 1 rnd, knit 2 rnds, purl 1 rnd, knit 3 rnds, purl 1 rnd. Now work eyelet round: (yo, k2tog) around. Purl the next rnd. Now work following the chart.

Great Masterwort

I often walk through our wonderful Hermelin Park here in Luleå. The names of the various plants are identified with little signs. One plant is called Great Masterwort. It was the perennial of the year in 2005 and usually gets around 19¾-27½ in / 50-70 cm high.

Knitting Instructions: Using the two-color method, CO 60 sts (see Techniques, page 10).

Star White

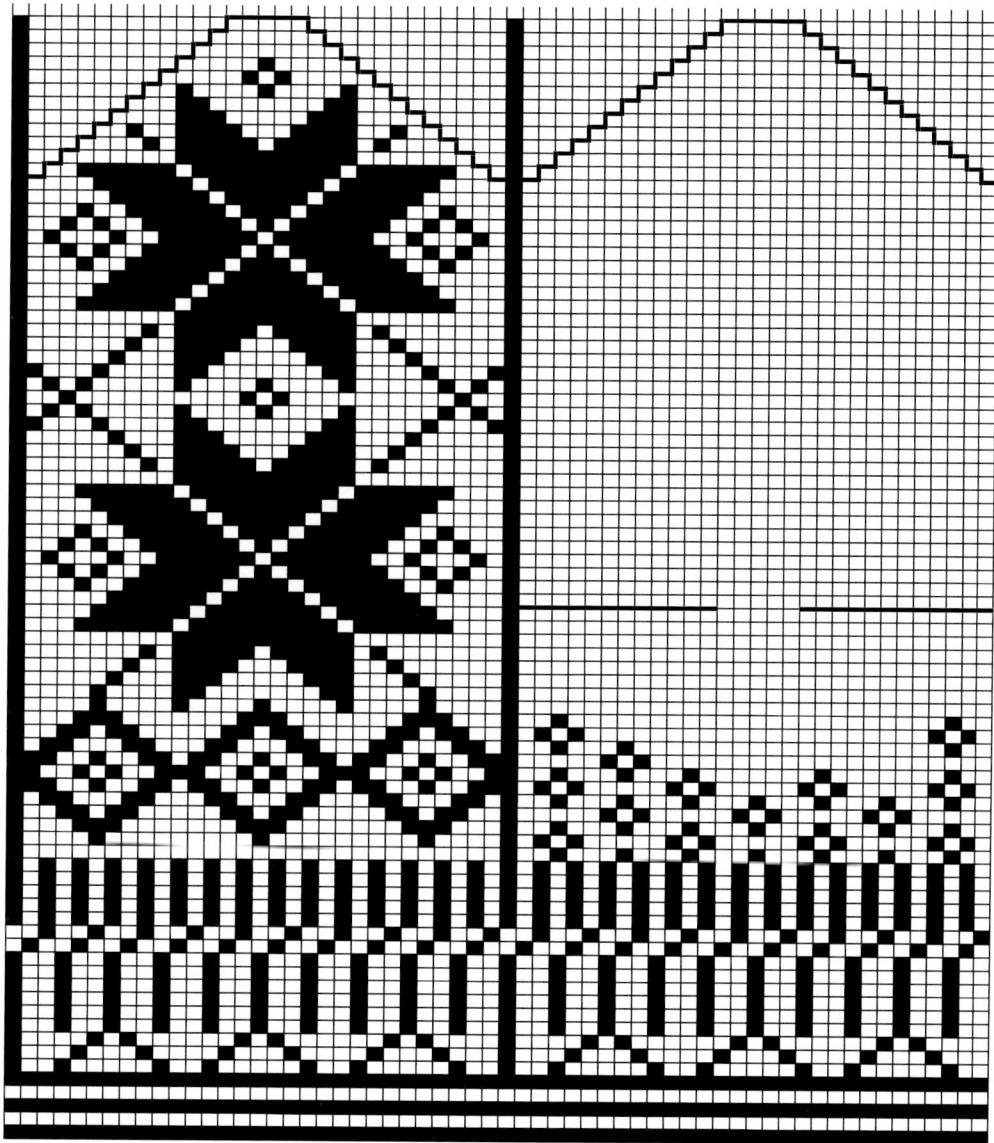

Knitting Instructions: Using the double start method, CO 60 sts, holding the black strand over your index finger (see Techniques, page 11). Knit 6 rnds of garter stitch (alternating knit and purl rounds) and then work following the charted pattern.

Kalix River Mittens

There are two main towns in the Kalix River valley. One is Kalix, near the coast, and the other is Överkalix, about 48 miles / 80 kilometers up the river. I designed two pairs of mittens inspired by the well-known musician and crafter Vifast Björklund. He was considered very knowledgeable even in that textile-rich area.

The Kalix town church, Sweden's northernmost medieval church.

Mittens from Kalix

The design inspiration for these mittens is an old pattern on a cap knitted by Vifast Björklund. The cap is in the collection of the Nordic Museum in Stockholm.

Yarn: 3-ply (sportweight) wool yarn: red and black

Needles: U.S. size 2-3 / 3 mm: set of 5 dpn

Right Mitten

Cast On: With the red and black yarn in your left hand and needle in your right hand, work long-tail cast-on as follows: Make a slip knot loop with both colors held together and place loop on needle. Hold the red yarn around your index finger and the black yarn around your thumb as for long-tail cast-on. CO 44 sts. Divide sts over 4 dpn and join, being careful not to twist cast-on row.

Lower Edge: After completing cast-on, bring both yarns to the front between the first and last needles. Work chevron braid:

Rnd 1: Alternating red and black, purl every stitch, keeping both strands on the RS throughout and bringing the next color *over* the previous one.

Rnd 2: Work as for Rnd 1, with red over red and black over black, but bring the new color *under* the previous one.

Now work following the chart.

Note: The charted pattern begins with 2 rnds red. On Rnd 34, on needle 3, k1 and then work the next 9 sts with a smooth, contrast color waste yarn. Place the 9 sts back on needle and work in pattern. Continue in pattern for 28 more rounds and then begin top shaping.

Top Shaping: The top is formed with the flat shaping, decreasing at each side (see Techniques, page 10). Work decreases on alternate rounds for 4 rounds and then decrease on every round until 8 sts remain. Cut yarn and bring end through rem stitches; pull tight and weave in ends on WS.

Left Mitten
Work as for Right Mitten but place thumbhole on dpn 2, 1 st in from the side.

Thumb: Carefully remove waste yarn from thumbhole. Place the 9 + 9 sts each on a separate dpn. (K9 sts, pick up and knit 2 sts at corner) 2 times = 22 sts total. Work thumb in same pattern as for mitten hand for about 18 rounds. Shape thumb tip as for top of hand, decreasing on every round until 6 sts remain. Cut yarn and bring end through rem stitches; pull tight and weave in ends on WS.
Use yarn tails to stitch up any holes at corners on base of thumb and then weave in all ends on WS.

Braids and Tassels: Make two braids and two tassels and securely attach them to each mitten at lower edge opposite thumb.

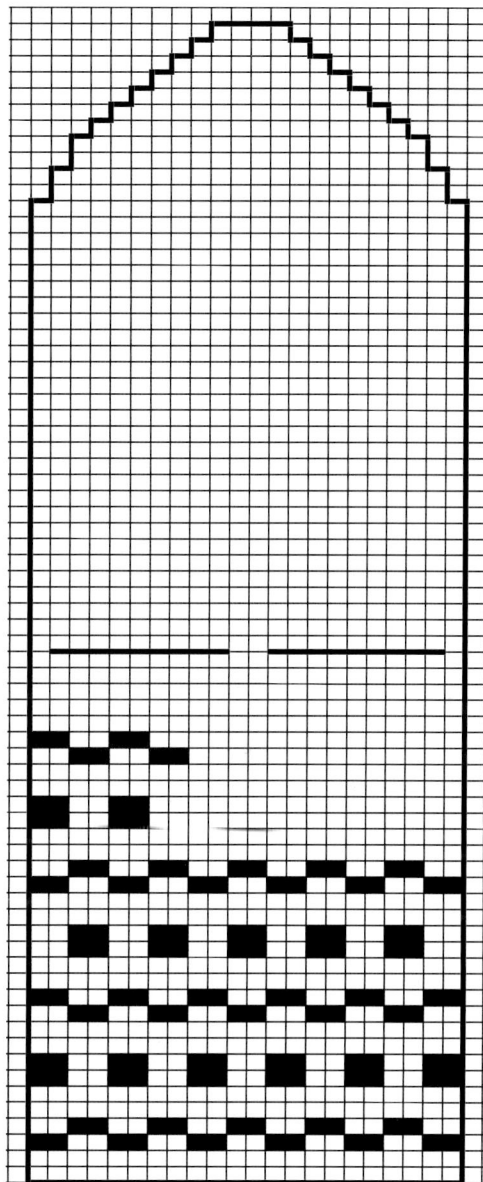

Interior of Martingården in Överkalix.

Mittens from Överkalix

These mittens were inspired by an old pattern on shoe ties woven by Vifast Björklund from Kangis outside Bränna in Överkalix.

Yarn: 3-ply (sportweight) wool yarn: red and black
Needles: U.S. size 2-3 / 3 mm: set of 5 dpn

Right Mitten
Cast On: With the red and black yarn in your left hand and needle in your right hand, work long-tail cast-on as follows: Make a slip knot loop with both colors held together and place loop on needle. Hold the red yarn around your index finger and the black around your thumb as for long-tail cast-on. CO 44 sts. Divide sts over 4 dpn and join, being careful not to twist cast-on row.

Lower Edge: After completing cast-on, bring both yarns to the front between the first and last needles. Work chevron braid:
Rnd 1: Alternating red and black, purl every stitch, keeping both strands on the RS throughout and bringing the next color *over* the previous one.
Rnd 2: Work as for Rnd 1, with red over red and black over black, but bring the new color *under* the previous one.

Now work following the chart. The front and back are identical.
On Rnd 31, on Ndl 3, k1 and then work the

next 9 sts with a smooth, contrast color waste yarn. Place the 9 sts back on needle and work in pattern. Continue in pattern for 28 more rounds and then begin top shaping.

Top Shaping: The top is formed with flat shaping, decreasing at each side (see Techniques, page 10). Work decreases on alternate rounds for 4 rounds and then decrease on every round until 8 sts remain. Cut yarn and bring end through rem stitches; pull tight and weave in ends on WS.

Left Mitten
Work as for Right Mitten but place thumbhole on Ndl 2, 1 st in from the side.

Thumb: Carefully remove waste yarn from thumbhole. Place the 9 + 9 sts each on a separate dpn. (K9 sts, pick up and knit 2 sts at corner) 2 times = 22 sts total. Work thumb in charted thumb pattern for 18 rounds. Shape the tip as for top of hand, decreasing on every round until 10 sts remain. Cut yarn and bring end through rem stitches; pull tight and weave in ends on WS.

Use yarn tails to stitch up any holes at corners on base of thumb and then weave in all ends on WS.

Hemavan Valley.

Víví

I used 13 different shades of yarn for these mittens.

Knitting Instructions: CO 60 sts and work lower edge:
Work 6 rounds of garter stitch (alternate knit 1 rnd, purl 1 rnd). Next, knit 2 rnds, purl 1 rnd.
Now work 2 rnds k1, p1 ribbing, and then knit 2 rnds.
Work the rest of the mitten following the charted pattern.

Acknowledgments

It is interesting and fun to publish a book, but one can't do it alone.

I want to thank everyone who phoned or mailed me with every question possible about knitting, patterns, and yarn. There have been many conversations — some of them quite long! — that have spurred me on and inspired me to continue.

I have long been interested in the accomplished women who knitted to support themselves and their families and who furthered our knitting traditions and handed them on to the younger generations. Many created new patterns and techniques that have brought the rest of us great happiness.

For this book, I've received a great deal of help from Carin Bremberg and Kajsa Bremberg who told me about and provided pictures of Jenny Bremberg, one of the women who spread the Arjeplog mitten pattern. Britt-Marie Wallbing, through the Porjus Archive Committee, helped considerably by bringing out photos and facts about the knitter Maria Juni. The Norrbotten Handcraft Consultant Maud Ån, at Norrbotten's museum, contributed with stories about Lisa Zetterström and her special cottage in Vistasdalen. Göran Wallin photographed Lisa's cottage and Maud with one of the few textiles that had been saved from the cottage at the last minute.

My husband Leif Larsson has supported me, by, among other things, proofreading and drawing illustrations for the book. Finally, my publisher Christina Snell-Lumio spurred me on and, as always, did an excellent job on the book's layout.

A big THANK YOU to everyone!

Solveig Larsson